# The Power of ONE!

## How to Impact Lives by Changing Your Own.

By
Tanya T. Morris

© Power of the T Enterprises 2015

*Dedicated to my friend and mentor*

*J. Wyatt Mondesire.*

# Table of Contents

*Introduction — The Power of One* ..................vii
*Chapter 1: Stewardship* .............................. 1
*Chapter 2: The Call* .................................... 9
*Chapter 3: Discouraged to Be an Encouragement* .... 17
*Chapter 4: Blurred Lines* ......................... 25
*Chapter 5: Shift Happens* ........................ 33
*Chapter 6: Mentorship* ............................. 41
*Chapter 7: The Mentoring Merry-Go-Round* ............. 45
*Chapter 8: Give and Grow* ........................ 55
*Chapter 9: Hey Girl!* ................................ 65
*Chapter 10: Leadership: Agents of S.H.I.E.L.D.* ....... 83
*Chapter 11: The Advocacy Agent* ............................. 87
*Chapter 12: The Frankford Fighter*............................ 95
*Chapter 13: A Leader's Leader* ............................. 101
*Chapter 14: The Mother of Reinvention* .................. 107
**BONUS CHAPTER:** *Resources & More!* ................ 113

# The Power of
# ONE

*"And the glory which You gave Me I have given them, that they may be one just as We are one"* **John 17:22**

## The Power of One

"And the glory which You gave Me I have given them, that they may be one just as We are one" John 17:22. Jesus greatest desire was for the disciples and future believers to become one. For them to be unified as a powerful witness to Gods love.

The Power of One is the innate, spirit-led desire and willingness of one person through his or her presence, action and life to impact the lives of others. The Power of One can be genuinely experienced through stewardship, mentorship and leadership. But what makes it powerful is the inexplicable way that your life is changed, while you are sharing your story and extending yourself to others.

One is not only a singular number, but it also represents unity. The power of one can be best demonstrated through the willingness and desire of individuals who work together toward a common goal. That common goal is accomplished through stewardship, mentorship and leadership. When those three are unified in a group, the impact could potentially change the course of a neighborhood, community, city, state or even a nation. Together, they produce a movement. A movement is the greatest example of the Power of One. Throughout history, we see the impact of what happens when groups unify for one cause, one mission and one purpose. From the civil rights movement, to the charismatic movement, to one of todays movement called the occupy movement; change winds blow when people come together.

The Occupy movement became the international branch of the Occupy Wall Street movement that protests against social and economic inequality around the world. Manfred Steger calls it the "global justice movement. Occupy protest spread over 951 cities across 82 countries and over 600 communities across the United States. This movement represents the Power of One.

## *Black Lives Matter*

"Black Lives Matter" is another powerful movement that represents the Power of One. Now there are varying opinions as to whether or not Black Lives Matter constitutes as a movement or even if it has an agenda. But like so many movements that were birthed out of pain or injustice, Black Lives Matter which actually began as a hashtag; following the deaths of Trayvon Martin, Michael Brown, Eric Garner and Freddie Gray to name a few, raised the level of consciousness and called attention to the issue of police brutality. Does it matter that the victims were Black? Of course it does!

Black Lives Matter symbolizes a Movement and The Power of One. Why? It called attention to an issue that had the ability to rally and unite a diverse group of people around a common cause globally. What a great feeling it is to be part of a life changing movement exercising great purpose igniting change. I attended a conference; Judy Wicks, who I consider one of the greatest social entrepreneurs of our lifetime and who is

## The Power of One

widely considered the mother of sustainability, talked about the impact we can have in our own communities at the Social Impact Conference I attended. And what she said was true and powerful "We don't have to take our money and talents outside of our communities," Judy said. "Social change begins with non-cooperation with an evil system. Well, that takes a movement, unified in mind and spirit to make a difference in our community, our city and ultimately our world."

Remember, The Power of One is the innate, spirit-led desire and willingness of one person through his or her presence, action and life, to impact the lives of others.

### *Civil Rights Movement*

While channel surfing one day, I was also writing a paper for my MBA class, and landed on Selma, the critically acclaimed film depicting the life of Martin Luther King and the Civil Rights movement. My surfing took me to the scene at the Edmund Pettis Bridge, after "Bloody Sunday." For those of you who are not familiar with Bloody Sunday, during January and February of 1965, Martin Luther King, and the Southern Christian Leadership Council led a series of demonstrations to the Montgomery, Alabama County Courthouse. On February 17, 1965, protester Jimmy Lee Jackson was fatally shot by an Alabama state trooper. In response, a protest march from Selma to Montgomery was scheduled for March 7. When protesters refused to disperse, state troopers unleashed teargas and waded through the crowd with Billy clubs. Over fifty people were hospitalized as the world watched in horror that day. Later

## Tanya T. Morris

King called for civil rights leaders to come to Selma for a second march and pressure congress to pass the Voting Rights Act. As I watched the second march, I began to think what kind of relationship Dr. King had to have with God on that historical day as he stood on that bridge? Alabama State Troopers in front of them, and hundreds of people were behind Dr. King awaiting his next move. I could not help but think about Kings level of discernment as he stood on that bridge possibly thinking "this could be a trap", and ultimately deciding to turn around knowing hundreds of people would follow him as they internally questioned his decision to retreat. You see, the power of one isn't about ego or control; its servanthood and being able to relinquish your own ambitions, your own dreams and interest, for the betterment of others. But here's the powerful part, when you give up those things, you change and mature in character at the same time. In that singular pivotal moment, future leaders were birthed; John Lewis; Andrew Young; Hosea Williams; and many more we don't know by name. More importantly, that pivotal moment changed the lives of those men and women on that bridge who became great leaders in civil rights history. That's powerful! Look back over your own life and think about a singular moment or an individual who changed or shaped the way you viewed the world. It may have been a schoolteacher, a neighbor, an enemy or even the person who got the promotion instead of you. Maybe it was the civil rights movement, or some other cause you believed in enough to get involved. Whatever or whoever it was, now it's our time, our turn to impact lives and we can do it if we unify as one!

# ONE
# Stewardship

*Well done, good and faithful servant;  
you have been faithful over a few things,  
I will make you ruler over many things.*

## The Power of One

**I**f you are going to be that individual who impact lives, you must be a good steward of whatever God puts in your hand to accomplish.

So, "what exactly is stewardship?" And, "what does it mean to be a good steward?" Stewardship is oversight and protection of something or someone worth caring for and preserving. When I think of stewardship, I think about parenting. Parents have been given the great responsibility to shape and mold the lives of their children. Parenting is not just about providing care, security and love. No, it's much deeper than that. Our children are on loan to us by the Lord. This is real (*stewardship*). Whether you are a product of marriage or of illegitimacy, God ordained your birth.

So much of what we learn, if not everything, began in our childhood. How many of us, especially women, as we matured, saw the reflection of our mothers when we looked in the mirror, cooked in the kitchen or disciplined our own children? Sometimes I just shake my head and smile when I say something and hear my mother. It's fascinating how we adopt the mannerisms, attributes of another person.

Introducing and instilling values, beliefs and morals in our children can and will carry them for life! When I look at my sons, I see so much of myself, but I also see their uniqueness. Certainly our children are worth our oversight and protection. When I look at Isaiah I see my love, passion, work ethic, faith and commitment. As much as he has tried to pursue a business career, when he graduated from Community College of Philadelphia his first position was as an out-of-school-time camp counselor. He has always loved children, and young people have always been drawn to him. I've seen infants go to Isaiah when they wouldn't go to anybody else. In addition to his love, he is passionate about being an example to boys who are being raised by single parents, as he was.

When I look at Jeremy, I see my gifts. He's an excellent speaker and writer; he researches and studies film and television like a true artist. And even though he took the long way around to find his career as an actor, writer, producer, he's doing it.

Last year he starred in his first play, he's been a spokesman for the Southeastern Transportation Authority, Campbell's and Microsoft. He just produced a short film and he was an extra in *How To Get Away With Murder*.

Scripture proclaims, "Train up a child in the way he should go, and when he is old, he will not depart from it." (**Proverbs 22:6**). When most look at this verse, it is generally from a spiritual perspective. However, train up in the Hebrew text means to dedicate, to inaugurate, which makes it the parents' responsibility to be and remain dedicated to the rearing of the child. Our children are on loan to us by the Lord. This is real (*stewardship*). Whether you are a product of marriage or of illegitimacy, the bible says God ordained your birth.

## The Power of One

> *"My substance was not hid from thee, when I was made in secret and curiously wrought in the lower parts of the earth"* ***(Psalm 139:15)***
> *Thine eyes did see my substance, yet being unperfect: and in thy book all my members were written, which in continuance were fashioned, when as yet there was none of them. (Verse16).*
> *God knew you before you were born!*

Even though he's not my natural son I have known Christian Weatherbe since he was a boy. His grandfather was not just one of my favorite preachers, but someone I tried to emulate in my teaching. Bishop Johnny Weatherbe was teaching purpose way before most ever heard of Myles Munroe. I was a member of Yesha Ministries Worship Center and Bishop Weatherbe was the pastor of Agape Love Ministries. Our churches fellowshipped often and we attended an annual conference together. I watched Christian grow up and even though I didn't spend a lot of time with his mother, he became like a son to me from hanging out with Jeremy and Isaiah and other kids during the annual conference. I am as proud of him as I am Jeremy and Isaiah.

Christian is a model, an entrepreneur,
and social media expert.

His greatest accomplishment has been his organization The Refreshed Life.

Every Thursday for the last year and half Christian organized volunteers, millennial like him to distribute peanut butter and jelly sandwich, a snack and bottled water to homeless throughout the city of Philadelphia.

In 2015 they fed ten thousand and the 2016 goal is to help low-income, impoverished communities worldwide and feed 100,000. The power of one is about giving, giving back and paying it forward. What would happen if everyone did one simple thing to contribute to society like Christian? Imagine the impact it could have on our community, our city and possibly even our world.

Christian Weatherbe is proof that we are all worth caring for and preserving. And stewardship is the way that happens.

Stewardship operates in three phases: **dedication, management and discipline**. Stewardship begins with dedication. Dedication is being committed to purpose. Purpose says that regardless of how it looks, I am dedicated to seeing it through; It means that I am dedicated and committed to the person, money and activity that I have been assigned to oversee and steward. Without dedication, the seed of stewardship will never become fruitful.

The next phase is Management. Management requires faithfulness. The parable of the talents was a test of faithfulness. Each servant was given a talent; one, two and five. Two of the servants traded their talents and received double, but the other buried his in the ground. Talent not only represents money, but also translates as weight. What is that thing that weighs heavily on your heart? The thing that wakes you up in the morning and that won't let you sleep at night? How are you managing it?

## The Power of One

I absolutely love event planning; recruiting powerful speakers, finding exceptional entertainment, and marketing. However, what I enjoy the most is managing the event day and ensuring the attendees get what they paid for and have a good time. When I plan an event, I do it knowing that I am responsible for being a good steward of the vision placed in my hands. Burying my talent in the ground is unacceptable knowing that the Father is expecting a return.

The servant who buried his talent was called wicked and lazy! He failed to manage (steward) correctly the talent he was given. (*Mathew 25:18*)

Last is Discipline, discipline is training expecting to produce a specific character, pattern, or behavior. It is a regimen that develops or improves a skill. Discipline produces growth. I have the utmost respect and appreciation for those who exercise regularly because it requires a level of discipline to exert that kind of energy daily, weekly and on a consistent basis.

There's a group called Black Girls Run in Philadelphia. Every time I see a colleague of mine, she is running, geared up with sneakers, towel, and water, preparing for her next race. She is consistent. She is passionate about fitness and running. Beyond that, she is disciplined. Being a good steward will require discipline. You must be disciplined in your giving, your receiving, your time and your speech. Discipline is self-control, and in order for you to be a good steward, you must be disciplined in every area of your life. Now that we have laid some foundations, lets continue to build in the proceeding chapters.

# TWO
# The Call

*When the why is clear,
the what will appear.*

## The Power of One

**For as long as I could remember, I heard my grandmother tell me that there was a calling on my life.** Going to church with her is one of my fondest childhood memories. We'd leave out Sunday and go from one service to another, praying for a friend in between, stopping at Gino's (which was then the outlet for Kentucky Fried Chicken) for some fried chicken before heading back to Screen Temple for evening service. During the week, it was no different. After playing all day and fighting with my uncle over who would wash the dishes, I was still made to go. Even when I cried, embarrassed because my friends were laughing, watching me go to church while they played hide and seek, basketball or tops, she'd ignore me and pull off saying, "You can't do what everybody else can do."

There were times when I misbehaved and she had to save me from one of my mom's belts, she would preface it with, "Tanya, why did you do that? You can't do what everybody else can do. Don't you know that by now?" Sure enough, the older I got, and the more lies I got caught telling, every time I tried to be slick or got into trouble, I heard my grandmother's voice saying the same thing; "You can't do what everybody else can do."

I could not get away with anything. The other thing that my grandmother always told me was that I was called. Called to do what? Preach? Me, really?

Sometimes I believed it, other times I just ignored it and kept doing what I wanted to do.

When I joined the Philadelphia Revival Temple, I had been at my previous church, Mount Airy Church of God in Christ, for six years. I joined the public relations ministry and attended services regularly. If the doors were open, I was there. My grandmother was the one who really encouraged me to attend the large church. While in attendance, I felt there was more for me to do. I could hear her say, "Tanya's called to preach." When she got sick, the dementia worsened and grand-mom was admitted into a nursing home. It was obvious that she would not get a chance to hear me preach.

All those years of telling me that I was called to preach, that I couldn't do what everybody else could do, and she would not get a chance to hear me yield to the call. I remember the morning she passed, and when the phone rang, I knew. I dreamed about a wedding that night. The next day, as my mom and her siblings planned the home going service, I could feel the Holy Spirit reminding me, pushing me to tell my family that they didn't need to ask Apostle Hausley, my mother's pastor at the time, or even Teresa, who grew up with us at Screen Temple Church to preach because I would preach her home going. Initially, they were surprised, especially my uncles. My mom only asked me one time if I was sure, I said yes. Besides, I knew where my grandmother was going, without a shadow of a doubt. Yes, we miss our loved ones when they pass, but as Christians we don't grieve the way the world grieves. I couldn't help but think maybe I should have accepted the call sooner.

Looking back on those countless conversations with my grandmother about being "called" to preach, I realized that it wasn't just a call to preach but a call to make a difference. A call to make an impact on those I came in contact with on a daily basis. That calling, requires us to share our lives with others in such a way that we leave a mark. Sharing your life and telling your story really isn't up to you because God owns the copyright to your story, to my story. Since God owns the copyright to your story, that means whenever He wants to share it, or use it, he will call upon it to be released. It's His call. Have you ever found yourself sharing or telling something about yourself to someone and you didn't really know why? Well that's God releasing an authorized version of your story for someone else's benefit and for His glory. I remember years ago when Jeremy and Isaiah were little and I was struggling on welfare, our gas or water had just been shut off. I was on the bus downtown when a lady got on in obvious pain. Her hand was shaking, she had bandages on and I saw and empathized with her pain. I began praying for her in my mind when she extended her hand. I prayed for her right there on that bus. I got off the bus crying. Here I was complaining about my life and situation, but God in His infinite wisdom and power decided to use me anyway. I could not believe it. I'm sure you've had similar situations, wondering why and how you were telling your story or sharing an experience with a perfect stranger. Now, I understand that it wasn't my story God owns the copyright.

This is God saying to you and I that I (God) reserve the right to use portions of your story, whenever I want and wherever I want, in order to help someone else.

Second Peter 1:10 says, "Because of this brethren, be all the more diligent (KJV) to make sure (to ratify, to strengthen, to make steadfast) your calling and election, for if you do this, you will never fall." (AMP). To ratify is to confirm by expressing or giving consent. I consented when I accepted Christ, and now, I am required to actively, practice, and share my story through the gifting of the Holy Spirit in the territory where I am called. You have a similar obligation to discover where or to whom you are called. The vocation is irrelevant, really, because God owns the copyright. And since He owns it, and there are people who may have similar situations, problems, and pains, you and I need to hear it. Keep in mind, that without pitfalls and problems resulting in change, you could not make an impact.

I am always writing. When I get an idea, whether it's for a sermon, a business, a marketing strategy, or workshop—sometimes even for someone else—it works, and weighs heavily on me all day and all night. Sometimes it takes days and nights until I get it all out. If it ain't on the page, it ain't on the stage. I have notebooks; journals full of outlines; sermons; programs; possible events; and affirmations. Often when I go back through my journals, flipping through pages looking for something else, the

## The Power of One

Holy Spirit will direct my attention to a note, "You forgot about that, didn't you?" Other times, seeing past ideas will invoke praise because it's already done.

In *The Best Man Holiday,* Jordan gives Harper an iPad with a mock cover for his next book, Lance's autobiography. Jordan wanted to bring him up to date, out of notebooks, and his reply was totally relatable: "Writing notes, seeing and feeling it on paper makes it real."

Never mind Oprah's favorite things. One of Tanya T's favorite things to give and receive is a journal! I know we're in the technological age of Dragon and other voice-activated dictation programs. I own an iPad. And I've tried to just type, but there's nothing like putting pen or pencil to paper. It makes the words jump off the pages. If you don't keep a journal, try it. Write your dreams, ideas, business plans, programs, goals, and let the Holy Spirit breathe on it. Then watch them come alive as you share your story, making your calling and election sure.

This is a clarion call to go make a difference. Make an impact on the lives of others by first changing your own. Changing your own life begins with a decision to be honest about where you are, and being willing to make the adjustments to move forward in every area of your life.

# THREE

# Discouraged to Be an Encouragement

*"but David encouraged himself
in the LORD his God."*

## The Power of One

**It was the first Sunday in December 2014.** The worship experience was good as always. Our worship leader began to exhort and share his testimony. His band had been offered a deal with Universal Music Group that included a $2 million advance. Listening, I had a mixed response. I knew we were to rejoice with them, but as he declared the difference between God's provision and God's blessings, my rejoicing quickly turned to discouragement.

In all honesty, thinking about others advancing in their careers, and observing them as they were being considered for television, and possibly launching a reality show, caused me to sink lower and lower.

"Does God want to bless me", I thought?

"When will it be my turn for promotion, and advancement"?

"Maybe I'm just supposed to be average."

At the time, I was unemployed, and waiting for a response about a position that I'd applied for, and really wanted.

I was also being supported by unemployment benefits, which were nearly one third of my monthly salary. I had applied for the Low Income Home Energy Assistance Program for the first time in nearly 10 years and owed my mother money. It was Christmas time; need I go on, and on, and on...? "Did God forget about me"?

Later in that same service, the soloist gave another testimony of how he had a rough year, had been out of work for a long time, and felt like God was not there. Now that was something relatable! He concluded that he had been asking God for a particular position, and honestly didn't trust God to do it. However, that day he got the call that the job was his. I couldn't help but feel, "When would I have a testimony"? I kept my head down for the rest of the service, played church with an occasional wave and Amen, but honestly, I don't remember a word that was said. I wouldn't let it penetrate my heart. I certainly didn't want to be encouraged. All I wanted to do was sulk. Other thoughts flowed through my head and the word of God was nowhere to be found. I'd just had my 48th birthday, and felt I should have been working on my retirement plan. Instead I was considering food stamps, feeling like I was in a time warp back to when my sons, Jeremy and Isaiah were children.

Although I knew my last position was grant-funded and was going to end, I was confident that I would get back to work soon. There's no way I would have thought, that I'd be in the position that I was in, that is, jobless, at this time in my life. What had I done to deserve this? Or not done. I was praying, fasting, and most importantly, giving.

## The Power of One

"I'm a tithe payer Lord", I thought to myself, "and I give sacrificially always". Was there something that I'd missed?

Despite the economy, despite the opportunities, despite everything that was going on, I knew that there was a top-flight position in my future. I had resumes out, I had a job coach, I was networking; I was doing everything that I knew to do. Yet I was greatly discouraged!

One of my favorite movies is **"It's a Wonderful Life"**. The film opens with a discussion in heaven where the angel Clarence is assigned to help George Bailey. When Clarence is given the assignment, he asks, "Is he sick?" The answer: "Worse, he's discouraged." While this is fictional, the point emphasized is that discouragement is worse than being sick! Throughout *It's a Wonderful Life,* George Bailey is faced with decision after decision that discouraged or dissuaded him from doing what he wanted to do, where he wanted to go, and who he thought he should have been. First his father dies when he prepares to leave for college and he must take over the failing Bailey Building and Loan. Later his brother Harry returns from college to take over the company but has a job offer from his father-in-law. George is stuck again; can't even go on his honeymoon because he has to bail out the business, and the community, following another crisis and on and on. Finally, the crisis that drives him to wish he were never born becomes Clarence's opportunity to show George, that he had in fact had a "wonderful life." If George had never been born, he would not have been there to save Harry when he fell in a frozen creek. Which meant Harry would not have gone to war and become a hero and saved lives. Old man Gower would have been a homeless, helpless drunk. Violet would have been a hooker, and his small town would have become Pottersville, a place of degradation and poverty, instead of a town filled with homeowners and thriving businesses. Mary, his wife, would have become an old maid, and he would have never had an opportunity to kiss his kids. After seeing the impact he had on the lives of so many, George saw that the trials, the disappointments, and the discouragements, were all for a purpose. Through it all, he still made an impact on everyone with whom he came in contact. But when you are discouraged, you can't see that. You don't see the change, or how others are growing, developing or becoming better because of you. Too often we don't realize that our mere presence blesses others.

It was Jan. 17, 2014. I had been laid off on April 16, 2013. Since then, I could count the interviews I'd had on one hand. Times had changed since being employed as the Communications and Outreach Coordinator at the Energy Coordinating Agency. In this new technological age, the personal touch in human resources has gone digital. Rarely, if ever, do you get phone calls for interviews or even rejection letters. They don't even send responses when they receive your resume, or updates on the status of the position. It's beyond disappointing. It's sad.

*Maya Angelou once said that "people will forget what you said, they will forget what you did, but they will never forget how you made them feel"!*

## The Power of One

I'd recently applied for a position that I thought was dead on.

It would allow me to continue to make an impact in the community, work with entrepreneurs, and also access the resources necessary for building *Gurlification*.

We will talk about *Gurlification* in later chapters. What made the lack of response especially difficult in this case, was that two former colleagues interviewed me. So I had two interviews, and no emails, and no response. Discouragement seemed to have won another victory!

Finally, on January 24, after being unemployed for nine months, I accepted the Community Liaison position at Turning Point for Children. Turning Points for Children, is a child welfare agency built on the foundations of wellness, safety, diversity and collaboration. Honestly, I was more relieved than excited. On many occasions it was still hard to accept, but at 48 I was still finding my way professionally. I was so excited about applying for a position at Goldman Sachs 10,000 Small Businesses, but so disappointed when the offer never came. My enthusiasm waned. I felt like accepting anything less was a setback, and was beneath me. Discouragement had shown it's ugly head again. The position I had taken was for less money; I was really hoping to move out of the nonprofit sector and plant my feet in the energy industry in some way. There were so many positions that I would have been excited to accept, not because of their salaries, but, I felt they would have made better use of my entrepreneurial spirit, and passion for economic development.

It felt like case management, even though it was community outreach in which I love. I knew at some point and in some way it would require being involved in the lives of people. It was PathWays PA, Women's Opportunities Resource Center and the Kintock Group all over again. My focus on making an impact had shifted from public service, to welfare to work and advocacy. Or had it?

Once again I had been discouraged to be an encouragement. As I began to see the opportunity to work and engage parents, and see this position as I saw many others. It became clearer that my entrepreneurial spirit would require oversight and foresight. As an outreach and communications expert, I know how to reach people and motivate them to be better. Undoubtedly, my entrepreneurial spirit would be as useful, and even more so in this role, than in any other. I was motivated to make a difference.

# FOUR
# No Blurred Lines

*Clarity, clarity, clarity!*

## The Power of One

**A** **few years ago Robin Thicke released the song "Blurred Lines."** Although it meant nothing to me, it implied that while a woman may be saying no, she really means yes. It is a message of misconception.

It was Christmas weekend 2010. I absolutely love Christmas and everything about it. Jesus Christ, Christmas movies, the parties, family dinner, Christmas breakfast, gifts, absolutely everything!

I was shopping for a few last minute gifts and decided to go to the JC Penny's outlet at Franklin Mills Mall. While returning to the car, I felt a sharp pain in my chest. It was like nothing I had ever experienced. I was scared and didn't know if I could make it to the car. I became dizzy and lightheaded. The pain had traveled up my arm. By the time I reached the car and got in, I could hardly breathe. I didn't know what was going on. "Should I try and drive to the hospital" "Call my mom" Or "Call 911"? All kinds of things were running through my head. Instead I sat there, praying silently, breathing slowly, thinking about my sons Jeremy and Isaiah, my mom, and my friends. I've heard people say how your life flashes before you. For me it was all a blurr. I did not want to accept at that very moment I may have been in trouble. At that time, every aspect of my life was blurry; my career, my family, my hopes and my dreams. As I continued to try to get myself together, by trying to catch my breath, I prayed the headache would at least subside, if not go away. I was unsure of what this incident even meant going forward. Was it a stroke? Maybe it was a heart attack. Whatever it was, it was blurry. It was a defining moment in my life. I told no one except my mother. It became clear that I needed to make some changes in my life. All change begins with being honest with yourself first, and then you can help someone else be honest about making changes in their own life.

Even though I felt better I couldn't forget what happened that day. The holidays had passed and it was time for my annual physical. I told my doctor what happened, she requested blood work. My heart rate was accelerated, blood pressure was a little high as well, and she referred me to the cardiologist with a preliminary diagnosis of a mild stroke. When you hear stroke you automatically think the worse. "What if it was a stroke?" "Will it happen again?" Why didn't I have the signs; mouth drooping, weak arm, difficulty speaking. I didn't know what to expect from the cardiologist.

I just knew I wanted to get there, get the examination, figure out what was going on, and take the next step if there were any. The test was general; EKG, stress test, the treadmill.

The cardiologist concluded that it was an isolated incident and not a stroke. Relieved, I still decided that I needed to make some changes in my diet and began to exercise, but I needed to do what worked for me. Since my basketball days I have never been a gym person. I have friends who are fanatical about the gym, not me. I like to walk and I have grown fond of yoga and even line dancing. You have to do what works for you.

I lost ten pounds, but more importantly I felt better. I never thought any more about what happened until October 2015. I was working at Turning Points for Children, a year and a half had passed, and by then I was miserable. Again, I never wanted to be in child welfare.

I enjoyed community work but after years of running around Chester, Delaware, Montgomery counties and Philadelphia, the thrill was gone. I reluctantly accepted the position at Turning Points despite not wanting to learn another industry.

Every industry has its own acronyms; policies, procedures, structure, and operations, I just didn't want to go through that again. Ironically, Turning Points was a child welfare agency, and I had to learn about The Department of Human Services culture.

Its terminology, services, the trauma, and the difference between foster and kinship care. I made the best of it.

I even made some great connections, and learned some things I didn't know about Frankford, one of the oldest neighborhoods in the city of Philadelphia.

Most importantly, I gained a new respect for social workers, especially case managers. I had been a case manager, but child welfare case management is on another level! The future and lives of children are in their hands. In addition, they are dealing with families and administrators some of which don't have a clue. The other half doesn't care. In the movie Parenthood with Steve Martin, a young Keanu Reeves tells his girlfriends mom about his father and how he would wake him up by flicking a lit cigarette at him to make him breakfast. As he continued to describe his abusive father Tod played by Keanu Reeves said "You know Mrs. Buckman, you need a license to drive a car, heck you even need one to catch a fish, but they'll let any a... hole be a father". These are the kind of people or worse that social workers deal with every day. Unfortunately, you can't turn that kind of person into a good parent overnight. Because, the first change that must take place is a heart change and only God can do that!

The heart has a funny way of letting you know it's being stressed or it needs relief. I was miserable, but I did my job. I also wanted out in the worse way! I was getting ready for work downstairs watching *"A Different World"*, sent a few emails, and then it happened. Heart starts racing, I felt light headed, I couldn't catch my breath, and felt like I was going to pass out. *Blurred lines again.* I sat down on the sofa, took a few deep breaths, walked to the kitchen to get a glass of water, then back to the sofa until I could get myself together. I had to drive and go to work, so I got in the car thinking it had passed, but there it was again. Finally I called my mom and here was my question, "Mom am I going to have to pay the $200 co-pay for going to the emergency room"? After I explained what was wrong, and she finished yelling for me to take my butt to the hospital, I drove myself to

## The Power of One

Chestnut Hill Hospital. I managed to park and basically crawled into the ER. They got me on a table quickly, gave me an injection to slow down my heart rate, and I was admitted. Shocked and irritated, I couldn't help but think *"my streak of not being admitted to the hospital was broken at ten years."* When the cardiologist on duty came to see me, his first question was if this had happened before. I hate the hospital! I hate nurses coming in and out of the room all night. And I hate having my blood taken all day and night. I hate everything about it.

Dr. Diaz explained that I had a condition called "Supraventricular tachycardia" (SVT) meaning that from time to time your heart beats very fast for a reason other than exercise, high fever, or stress. For most people who have SVT, the heart still works normally to pump blood through the body. SVT may start and end quickly, and you may not have symptoms.

SVT becomes a problem when it happens often, lasts a long time, or causes other symptoms. It can also be caused by certain medicines. I had a cold for almost ten days when the attack happened and I was using a nasal spray. Some nasal sprays contain steroids, which can cause your heart to race, and I was using it everyday. I stayed in the hospital overnight. It was a month before my book "The Power of One" was to be released. I was nagging my editor and my web designer was AWOL. I also had party planning, and graduate school ahead of me. There was a lot going on and I needed to go! I was prescribed a pill to take daily, which I did, but I declared that God had to heal me because I refused to be bound to a pill.

One morning I woke up and realized I was running out of medicine. I needed to contact Dr. Diaz for the refill and I kept forgetting. I was transitioning to leave my full-time job, and making moves figuring out my health insurance plans and I never got around to it. Three months later I was walking more and feeling great. Again I told my pastor that I refuse to be bound to a pill and I meant it. I haven't taken a pill since and at my follow up visit with Dr. Diaz he agreed that was fine.

*Offenses Must Come*

As stated earlier Blurred Lines is saying one thing and meaning something else. While this may happen often the flip side is when you are honest with someone, or maybe you're just having a simple conversation, and later you find out that the person was upset or offended. But here's the thing: The person was not offended by what you said, but by the way that you said it. This is something that's been said to me more than once. And I never really understood and ironically I was offended.

I would say to myself, "how can the way the message was delivered have more weight, more impact, than what was said? I would rather you say, "Listen, you really hurt my feelings," or, "That was hard for me to hear," than for you to say, "It was how you said it." As I said earlier, intent is important and it should be tempered with love, metered by truth. There must be tact and truth. And when those two characteristics are aligned timing will reign and there will not be any blurred lines.

# FIVE
# Shift Happens

*When you make up your mind to change, you remake history!*

## The Power of One

**E**very **relationship experiences a shift.** Shift happens when two people are no longer in the same place spiritually, emotionally, professionally or personally.

Shift usually happens in relationships for one of three reasons, either a lack of communication, the season of that relationship has come to an end or lastly, growth. First, let's look at the failure to communicate.

Silence doesn't necessarily mean that someone is angry or frustrated- nor does silence mean that you should go running after the person for an explanation. But, sometimes there's simply nothing else to say. In the words of Mars Blackmon, Spike Lee's character in *'She's Gotta Have It',* "When everything is said and done, there's nothing else to say or do!" I know for me, when I get quiet, it is a clear indicator that it's time to move on. Sometimes you get to a point in a relationship—I'm not talking about marriage, I'm talking about mentoring, friendships, work, classmates, homies and home girls—when you have to recognize that the relationship is going through a shift. There comes a point when one or both parties have nothing else to offer, it is what it is, so you don't have to force it. This is especially true in mentoring. You must know when the apex has been reached and when the protégé must take responsibility for the deposit. A word of advice, you can't keep pouring and watering someone and never see any growth or fruit.

I like to compare relationships to bank accounts. You would never make a deposit to your account or receive direct deposit from your employer and not inspect it, plan how to use it or invest it. Some of us even know how we are going to spend our paycheck before it even gets to the account. We should treat the information and knowledge that others share with us the same way, by taking responsibility for it and putting those resources to action. I am very clear about my purpose in the mentoring relationship; to provide insight, share experiences, resources, and present options. Finally, it is the protégé's decision to engage. That's The Power of One! As the mentor or the experienced person, in any relationship we must embrace our role and accept the fact that we can only do but so much. The responsibility lies within the protégé; this person may be a student, a child, or a subordinate that you have invested your time, tears, talent and truths within.

Shift indicator number two, "Growth." How many times have you said or heard someone say, "*We just grew apart.*" That was a shift. I believe that relationships were designed by God to add value to our lives. Every person to whom you are connected should be adding value to your life. Let's be honest, do we really need more friends? When I go into a new business relationship or company, I'm not looking for friends. I am all about the work, and how we can accomplish our goals in order to maximize success. I have plenty of friends, and I love them all, some are still a part of my life and others have shifted. In both cases, the love remains.

Another place where relationships shift, is in our profession or employment. This shift can be most rewarding. One of my most memorable shifts was working as a job developer/case manager for The Women's Association for Women's Alternatives (WAWA) or what is now PathWays PA. My supervisor at the time was Erika Loperbey; we became great friends. Our offices were in Swarthmore. While it was a long drive, I liked working in Delaware County.

When I left Swarthmore to go to Philly and have a micromanager for a supervisor, it was needless to say, challenging. The constant calling into the office, the cell phone calls, the sitting in on presentations, it all became a bit much.

The problem as I see with micromanaging is that it can potentially hinder growth. You must let people make their own mistakes in order to grow and learn. That's how you empower your staff to be creative, by buying into the company's vision, and ultimately becoming successful.

A year later I accepted a newly created position as Communications and Outreach Coordinator back in Swarthmore. I was ecstatic!

My first day on the job, my director Jane Elam and I went to the kick off for the Campaign for Working Families. Outreach was still relatively new to me, and I was somewhat intimidated by my environment. We went to the University of Pennsylvania, and there were at least 100 people there, including the mayor and partner agencies.

I began thinking, "I'm responsible for the outreach, really?"

I asked Jane for direction on what to do, and who to see. She kindly handed me a stack of flyers and said,

"Figure it out."

I made plenty of mistakes that first year, none of which I would take back. I enjoyed going to work every day, learning about income taxes, the Earned Income Credit, what it meant to low income families, and how to teach them to take responsibility for their financial future. Twelve years later, the majority of programs and operations the campaign employees use today, were tested, tried and implemented during those early years when we were just figuring it out. Growth comes from making mistakes, and you have to let people go through their process.

Shift indicator three is "Season."

"To everything there is a season. A time for every purpose under heaven." (Ecclesiastes 3:1). This is the big one when it comes to relationships and the shift. We must understand some if not most relationships are seasonal. We come into each other's lives at a particular time for a particular purpose. The reason why we need to understand and accept this fact is because we, especially women, try to hold onto people, male and female. Just because you may have grown up with an individual, doesn't mean that person is to remain part of your life forever. You may be mature, settled and have a career, while she still lacks ambition. That's a shift.

## IMPACT ACTIVITY

You can't just talk about making an impact- you have to do it. Being a good steward requires faith. Here's the first activity in the three stewardship areas; talent, tithes, and time.

### *TALENT*

Think of something that comes easy to you, that you can do without thinking about it. That's your talent. Write it down, and begin to think of ways that you can impact lives with your talent.

### *TIME*

*"Procrastination is the thief of time, collar him." — Charles Dickens*

Write down your three most pressing issues. Then consider what putting those things off has cost you personally, professionally, financially or spiritually. Take the step toward turning it around by attaching a time to them.

### *THE TITHE*
*A tithe is 10% or a tenth.*

Financial planning advises giving 10% to charity, 10% to savings and live on 80%. Now that's probably not realistic for most of us try this: Commit 10% of your income monthly, to something other than yourself. Write it down, and keep track of it.

# SIX
# Mentorship

*You can't reach out,
until you reach within.*

## The Power of One

**Mentoring is walking with a person through transition in order to discover God's divine purpose.** The main ingredient in the mentoring relationship is, virtue. It is a divine miraculous power, ability or force that activates an exchange. It is the exchange of virtue and divine power that can occur in mentoring and in coaching. Faith then activates virtue and virtue destroys bareness.

Faith in the person you believe has experience, information and resources that can change or impact your life. When the woman with the issue of blood came to Jesus, she activated her faith; she believed that He had the power to heal which thereby caused virtue to be released! When you have faith in the mentoring process virtue is released without permission! She didn't ask Jesus if she could touch Him or if He would heal her. No, she just believed, and virtue was released. Have you ever been with someone, a mentor, teacher or wise sage, and in a normal conversation his or her words began to impact you in a way you didn't think possible?

You received information, instruction, encouragement and power until you were full, and didn't know where to start applying what you just received. That was virtue being released into your life! You didn't ask for it, you simply believed the person had something to offer and bang! Virtue was released. When faith is present and the situation is right; virtue will be released without permission. There is also a virtuous exchange.

For a long time, many have thought mentoring and coaching were interchangeable. They are different. And the primary differences are the roles and responsibilities. In the mentoring relationship, the mentor is responsible. The mentor is responsible for accountability.

Holding the mentee accountable for completing assignments, follow-ups and applying the information you have given. In coaching, the client is responsible.

That person is responsible for scheduling the appointments and choosing the assignments. The client determines what he or she wants to learn as well as how and when to complete the assignments. Sometimes it can be challenging because I tend to use questions during mentorship and that's to push the mentee toward coaching and being totally responsible for his or her success. Sometimes it doesn't go that way, and it ends with mentorship and that's OK as long as mentees go from where they are to not only where they want to be but also where God would have them be.

# SEVEN

# The Mentoring Merry-Go-Round

*Circles...*
*"Out of my mind, that's where I'm*
*going/ trying so hard to deal with you.*
*It's not so easy trying to bare these changes/*
*Ooh, boy, that you're putting me through"*
*("Circles" by Atlantic Starr).*

## The Power of One

**I have learned something from every person I have mentored and vice versa.** The main thing I've learned is to forebear. There is a difference between forbearance and patience. I have learned patience primarily through relationships and work experience over the years. But forbearance is to patiently endure, refrain, or abstain, when subject to provocation. When most of us think of forbearance, we probably think about it as it pertains to student loans. When your loan is in forbearance, it's not just forgiven, but the lender is refraining from enforcing the penalty of interest, even though it has been provoked by a lack of repayment.

In the mentoring relationship, the opportunities to forbear are endless. There are times when you want to walk away, give up, fight or curse, when you want and even expect retribution, but for the good of the person, the relationship, you must choose to forbear in order to truly make a difference.

One of my first mentoring relationships started while I was the social service coordinator at The Kintock Group, a residential facility for offenders. I still remember his sweet yet sad face in our intake interview. Vernon was nineteen when he came to Kintock. I worked with him to go back to school and to get a job. When he left Kintock, and years later, he called me mom.

## Tanya T. Morris

After leaving the Kintock Group, I moved on to teaching at the Center for Literacy, which didn't last long. At that time, I was not equipped for the classroom. I took preparation for granted. Most of my students were mentally challenged therefore it required even more preparation. I felt as if I was babysitting. As a speaker and teacher, I learned the value and importance of preparing for the right audience. My skills needed some adjustments to meet this challenge.

While I was at the *"Center for Literacy"*, I was also freelancing for the *Philadelphia Tribune,* the *Daily News* and the *Sunday Sun.* I never wanted to write for newspapers, and freelancing is just too much work for too little money. You travel to event after event, chauffer celebrities to interviews, and deal with arrogant publicists. I just got tired of the rat race. Shortly after my mom's pastor recommended me for the position of Job Coach at *W.A.W.A.* in Chester, Pa, where Erica was my supervisor. It was during those first trips to Chester that I took my first ride on the mentoring merry-go-round began during those trips to Chester.

When I met Kia, she was in an abusive relationship. Her boyfriend threw her down the stairs and put her head through a glass window. Kia was a participant in the job training and mentoring program in Chester and I was the Job Coach. *Welfare to Work* programs were popping up all over the state when Pennsylvania became a "Work First State". This meant that in order to receive benefits, participants were required to enroll in a job-training program. We were housed in the former *Sacred Heart Hospital* in Chester, Pa. I didn't know I would spend a large part of my professional career in and around Chester Pa. Kia, like most participants, would come occasionally.

And like most participants, there were always issues with her kids, her family, transportation, or something.

The thing about mentoring, is you don't know that's what it is when it starts, it kind of morphs into a mentoring relationship. I just wanted to help and ensure that Kia kept her benefits, and eventually land a good job. I'm not exactly sure, at what point, I started going to the house where she was staying, or picking up the kids, or even taking her to services at *Yesha Ministries*, my church at the time. It just happened. It was year two of the program, and there was some rumbling that it would not be funded for a third year. I had been there one year, but I felt bad for Erika when it was not funded because she wrote the grant and started the program. It was the first time that a program Erika created had not been extended. As the two of us prepared to move on to other positions at Women's Association for Women's Alternatives, Erika said, "This program was just for Kia," there was no other explanation. We met all of our goals and participants were getting training and jobs. However, God always has another purpose and another plan. God can, and God will create a situation, an opportunity, and even a program just to get your attention and put you in position to make a difference.

Once the job training and mentoring program was officially over, Erika returned to the main office in Swarthmore, and I went to work for our welfare to work program in Philadelphia. It was there that I mentored Sara, Yaisha, Patricia and others. Some have stayed in my life, and as for others, I pray that they are better off than they were when we met. As welfare to work participants, attendance was mandatory.

If attendees missed more than one class, I'd call them.

If they were unable to be reached by phone, I'd do a drive-by. A drive-by is usually associated with violence or gang-related activity. However, the beauty of it is the element of surprise. A Tanya T. drive by is a surprise visit following a period of absence; It can happen at home, work or a known hangout. The purpose of the drive by is accountability. Accountability is critical for growth and success.

None of us have the right to be invisible, absent or missing. Accountability is giving someone permission to witness your life, the good, the bad and the ugly. No matter what you are going through or where you are when you go through it, accountability requires and demands that you check in.

Very few of the young women I have mentored had someone to hold him or her accountable for decisions, choices and actions. Nor have they held others accountable for how they have been treated or things they have said. Even after I returned to Philly I continued to take periodic trips to Chester. If Kia was not glad to see me, the kids sure were.

Case management was more than I could have ever imagined or expected. It's more than case management; you are managing that person's life! You're an advocate, a babysitter, financial advisor, chauffer, counselor, and mediator, I was burning out. As a result, when the opportunity to go back to the main office in Swarthmore became available I jumped at the chance. I had not heard from Kia in over a year when her ex called. Somehow she was in another bad relationship, pregnant with twins and living in a garage. I drove to Chester, and brought her to church. We ministered to her, she stayed a few days while I tried to find a Christian-based program for her, and we ended up at *Teen Challenge*. After lobbying for her to stay once, the director said it was not a babysitting service; that participants could leave when they wanted and that they must want to be there. Kia declined *Teen Challenge* and said, "No thanks, take me back to Chester".

Heartbroken, saddened and confused, I did just that. I couldn't understand how you would rather live in a garage, than sleep in a warm bed, get three meals a day and get clean. She even went to work with me. She connected with one young lady whose church had a program, *"Sobriety through the Word"*. She attended and loved it. It appeared we were on the right path until she got to Teen Challenge. But that's addiction. The next day I went to work, and the young lady asked, "Where's Kia?" I told her what had happened and said, "I just don't understand, she's hit rock bottom". Her answer to this day is one of the most profound things I've ever heard: **"But she hasn't hit *her* rock bottom."**

You can try to help someone as much as you want. Have the passion, even know and have the resources to help them get it together and get back to living and not just existing. But until that person has totally surrendered on their own, change will not come. Like the prodigal son when he started looking for something to eat in the pigs-pen, he realized that the servants in his father's house had three square meals, and more!

Luke 15: 16-17: "And he would gladly have filled his stomach with the pods that the swine ate, and no one gave him anything. But when he came to himself, he said, 'How many of my father's hired servants have bread enough and to spare, and I perish with hunger!" Going to the bottom of the barrel or the pigs-pen is where it takes most of us to come to ourselves. But it must be "your bottom," not the one assumed by someone else. So I got in my car and took her back to where I picked her up. Months later she gave birth to the twins, and moved in with their father's mother. It wasn't an ideal situation, and I always felt that the grandmother wanted to raise those twins as her own. After the first fall out with that family, Kia was calling me to pick her up. Back and forth it went, she stayed with me again for about a month, visiting the twins after she got off work. Kia had gotten a job at a diner. We got up at 5 a.m. and went to *Yesha* Ministries, my church at the time for 6 a.m. prayer. I had established a routine of dropping her off at the diner; I'd then go to my place of employment and sleep in the car until the secretary opened the office at 9am.

By this time, Kia's other children were in Children and Youth services. Kia had visits, and the conditions of her probation included that she do an inpatient treatment for another 90 days. It was after this, that I was very instrumental in getting her into *W.A.W.A's shelter*. Eventually, she transitioned into her own house with all the children, another high! These were the exciting good times of the merry-go-round. She found a good church home, and I felt really good. Mission accomplished!

Unfortunately, the need and desire for companionship and sex would get the best of Kia again.

While she has remained clean, she continues to toss in the wind. She resurfaces occasionally. Kia was never reunited with her older children who remained in the custody of the state until adulthood. Their father and his mother raised the twins. She has moved around from Chester, to Philly, to New Jersey. This is the mentoring merry-go-round. It goes around and around, highs and lows, and you do what you can, when and while you can. Mentoring is probably one of the most challenging relationships anyone can have outside of their family because of the emotional, spiritual, and mental investment that it requires.

The word mentor was inspired by the character "Mentor in Homer's Odyssey" in Greek mythology. Though the actual Mentor in the story is a somewhat an ineffective old man, the goddess Athena takes on his appearance in order to guide young Telemachus in his time of difficulty. The name Mentor was later adopted in English as a term meaning someone who imparts wisdom to, and shares knowledge with a less experienced colleague. However, the term became noteworthy for work between adults and children. Whether it's an adult/child relationship or a wise experienced adult imparting wisdom to a younger, less experienced colleague; it's a roller coaster ride filled with highs and lows. It offers one of the greatest opportunities to demonstrate the power of one. The sharing of knowledge with those less experienced, watching them apply that knowledge into growth, with people whom in turn impact others can be a powerful, fulfilling experience.

# EIGHT
# Give and Grow

*Change is hard when you fight.*
*It becomes easier once you surrender.*

## The Power of One

**I have learned something from every mentoring relationship firstly, as the mentor and secondly, from the standpoint of the protégé.** In both cases, knowing when to push and when to hold back are critical for growth. It's a give and take, not just to get your point across, but also to learn and grow. As a protégé there are times when you have to just sit and take it all in. It does not matter whether it's professional, financial, spiritual or educational. You can learn some of your greatest lessons by not only listening, but also watching and observing how your mentors operate and conduct themselves.

As a mentor, it's the same thing; you learn very quickly not only listening to what is being said, but also to what's not being said. You learn when to push forward, and when to stand your ground. Mentoring encompasses pouring, and depositing into the person what they are lacking in such a way that it empowers, motivates, builds, and leads them closer toward their God given destiny. When it's time to make the transition to coach, I get excited! I now get to make withdrawals from the investment in the lives God allowed me to deposits into. In order to give and grow in a way that impact lives and encourages change including your own, start with the spirit and the soul of the individual. There are two things here that I want to address; the Holy Spirit, and the human spirit. Galatians 5:16 says, "This, I say then walk in the spirit, and you shall not fulfill the lust of the flesh." The lust of the flesh is often seen as strictly giving into fleshly desires such as sex, drinking and partying. But the lust of the flesh includes anything done to satisfy one's selfish desires of that old sinful nature which is in opposition to the Holy Spirit. It is yielding to the sinful desire that is the problem. But how do you walk in the spirit and thus ensure that you do not fulfill the lust of the flesh? Ephesians 5:18-19 says *"speaking to yourself in Psalms and hymns and spiritual songs", fellowshipping with the Lord, giving thanks, and submitting yourselves to one another in the fear of God."*

In other words, it's through The Word, Prayer, Worship, Thanksgiving, and Accountability.

Putting into practice these spiritual things will cause you to forever walk in the spirit. That doesn't mean "church", but let me repeat, it is having spiritual conversations, prayer, meditation, anything and everything that builds up your resistance to the sinful nature of this broken down world, and its desires to do that which is unhealthy, unlawful, and unpleasant, all contrary to the law of God.

Only in the spirit can you identify the truth about yourself and begin to take steps toward change. Second, it's in the spirit that you can discern the needs of others and have an impact on the lives of others.

Third, and this is especially for the ladies, we must curb the "go-off." What does it mean to curb the go-off? Well, for me sometimes my "go-off" is to rebuke and ask questions later. Other times are just random you need to get yourself together!

And while I remain committed to the truth and telling the truth, every mistake, misstep and mishap does not equate a rebuke in response. Ladies, we are innately emotional, and those emotions often lead us to just go off! Many times, the "go-off" stems from our own inner struggles, pain and disappointments. And rather than address it, if someone crosses our paths, or brings up particular issues that are connected to those inner struggles, or disappointments, we go off!

As a mentor, there are times when the protégé may disappoint. Sometimes you see they are heading for a fall, or maybe they are not moving at the pace or in the direction you believe they should be for whatever reason; maybe its application, or they haven't taken advantage of an opportunity. It may be a decision you just don't agree with. Disappointment is different from anger or sadness. How many times have you said, "I'm not mad, I'm disappointed". I know I've said it more times than I care to remember.

My mom enlightened me, even when you have forgiven a person, and maybe you are not mad, the truth is, disappointment is still hurt. I would often say I was disappointed as a cop out for not being mad, all the while tears were running down my face. Disappointment hurts. And just like any other pain disappointment has to heal.

I know one thing that I do when I'm getting ready to go off, is rehearse over and over what I'm going to say, how

I'm going to say it and then just wait for the right time to go off! Let them have it! The problem is, that going off can sometimes cause folks to shut down. Everybody can't take you going off all the time, especially when they are doing the best they know to do. There are other times when "going off" is in order. Think about Jesus turning over the moneychanger's tables in the temple. Some people don't get moving, working, or doing what they need to do, until you go off!

One of the most volatile relationships I ever had was with a protégé. I still remember the day that Kay came into the Women's Opportunities Resource Center, late and loud. A smile so wide that it would light up any room. I was all ready to go when she came in after the receptionist asked if I could see one last person to enroll in the Family Savings Account Program. I was trying to get to Bible study, and I was already late, so I stood there for 10 minutes debating whether or not to see her. That's when the Holy Spirit said, "Help her, she's a chosen vessel unto me." Now what was I supposed to do with that information?

The calling on Kay's life was evident. She was charismatic, engaging and bright. But she was also hurt, abused, and had mental health issues related to misinformation and injuries from the abuse and life on the streets. Sometimes we can want to learn and acquire so much information that it's overwhelming especially when coupled with the poverty, disappointment, family estrangement, and drugs. The brain and emotions can only take so much. Kay became more than a protégé, she became a daughter. It was during that tumultuous time with Kay that I first realized I was a mentor. Everywhere we went, every event and every person we ran into that she knew; she introduced me as her mentor even though she called me mom. It was different and it was the first time I felt the investments I had made had real meaning. Truthfully, I didn't know what I was doing; I was just being obedient just helping out. If it was a ride, a resume, a resource, prayer, counseling.

I was simply following the Holy Spirit.

As with any other mentee, I tried to help Kay. She started attending church regularly, and I really began to see growth, but she was still so needy. She was living in a one-bedroom Philadelphia Housing Authority apartment. She had been in and out of school at the Community College of Philadelphia and on public assistance. Estranged from her mother, and siblings, at the root of her issues was the need we all have, to be loved. Kay clung to me like bees to honey. Calls in the morning during the day and calls in the evening. Sometimes I'd share the Word of God into her for hours. Kay was somewhat savvy financially. When we met she had a money market account and savings; that was a major accomplishment for a 22-year-old. But, she still needed and wanted direction.

She was trying hard to dissect mixed messages of Islam, Christianity, Israelites, and other religions, all in a quest for truth.

Even after she accepted Christ, she was still confused, thinking she had it all together and knew more than she did. Information without application will always lead to frustration. It's not enough to just learn and know. You must apply the learning in order to grow and develop.

Deep down I really believe that Kay wanted to be a better person, and she was doing the best that she could, all things considered. I continued to work with Kay exposing her to new opportunities, and introducing her to new people that I thought could help her reach her desired goals. She had an idea for a recycling business or community.

It was similar in form and content to the recycling initiative that the City of Philadelphia had launched, but she insisted it was different. When I started working at the Energy Coordinating Agency, it seemed ideal to help her figure it out. She was attending the Community College of Philadelphia, where she was struggling to finish her GED.

She finally got it and started volunteering at **ECA** (Energy Coordinating Agency). Unfortunately, Kay was always in crisis or survival mode! Balance is something we all need and should desire in our lives. Everything shouldn't be viewed as an emergency or a failure. Just because you didn't get it right the first time doesn't mean that you won't get it at all. For Kay, crisis or survival prevented her from dealing with her addiction and mental health issues.

Kay couldn't see that her addiction to marijuana ultimately led to her experimenting with the drug called wet (PCP). Sadly, young people were lacing it in marijuana. I was able to get her an appointment at a recovery

## The Power of One

program through a friend. She didn't make it through the week. Late for meetings, arguments with staff and of course it was everyone else's fault taking no responsibility for her actions. Despite all of these obvious issues, I continued offering help and assistance, and Kay would have her good days and bad. Sometimes as mentors we want more for the person than they do for themselves.

We push and push; we keep extending, despite the disappointments, struggles and obvious missteps.

You hope that one day, eventually, your mentees will see what you see. I really overextended my resources and myself when I decided to hire Kay as an AmeriCorps VISTA. Vista is an excellent program that offers many young people, the opportunity to get work experience through a paid internship. It paid participants $1,000 per month. They got to travel, and also got an award at the end of the term that could be used for education, or to repay a student loan. It started off well, but the issues were simply too much for Kay to overcome. She wasn't just late for work, there were no calls, and no shows.

Even then, I tried to let those inconsistencies slide, but, eventually co-workers began asking questions and looking at me like I was crazy; wondering why I was putting up with this kind of obviously unacceptable behavior.

Then one day we began having a series of arguments on different days, a major argument in the hallway, an argument on the street while leaving a meeting, and an argument in the car.

## Tanya T. Morris

The argument in the car is the one I regretted the most. I grabbed her, and the rage I saw that day was the one that let me know there were issues that I simply was not equipped to handle. And while I was hurt and upset, she acted as if nothing had happened. I couldn't even look at her for a week. Boundaries! Boundaries! Boundaries! Boundaries are the one thing that every mentoring relationship must have; there's no way around it. Boundaries both set by the mentor and the protégé. Honestly as much as I want my life to be an open book, and as much as I may want the protégé to be transparent, it doesn't always happen despite good intentions. The last time I saw Kay she hadn't come to work all week. She didn't show up for a major vending event and refused to take my calls. When I finally told my executive director what had happened, she was empathetic and encouraged me to move on, hire someone else, and get back to work.

Boundaries will protect you and the protégé. Boundaries can guide the relationship by establishing parameters beyond which neither is willing to go. If set properly, the relationship can blossom and there will be a positive outcome for all. Without boundaries, it's pretty much a free for all. And unfortunately, many of us learn that the hard way.

# NINE
# Hey Girl!

## The Power of One

**S**amia and I were never formally introduced. My earliest memory of her, besides shampooing my hair at Platinum Shears Salon and Barbershop, was at a hair show competition Naneke, a hair stylist entered in.

They did a skit on the evolution of musical girl groups from the Supremes, to Destiny's Child. It was years later when Naneke moved into her own salon, the Beauty Studio, that I found out Samia was a singer and songwriter.

Most conversations with the shampoo girl are casual, impersonal, and nothing deep.

I would get so annoyed sometimes when coming to get my hair done and she would say, "Hey girl." I would say to myself, "Doesn't she know I'm old enough to be her mother? "Who she think she talking to?" How come it's Ms. Cheryl and Ms. Yvonne, but I get, 'Hey girl." It used to burn me up. On top of that, when I asked Naneke to correct her, she thought it was funny.

"Oh, Tanya," Naneke said. "Stop being so serious, it's not disrespectful, she doesn't' mean anything by it, calm down."

When she says it now, I just laugh to myself and shake my head. "What are you laughing at?" she inquires. I just nod, shrug my shoulders and say "nothing," tickled at my private joke and how far we've come in our relationship.

The Truth is, you can only have but so many passing, informal, casual conversations with the shampoo girl.

It was during one of those casual conversations; probably about one of our favorite television shows, *Girlfriends* or *The Game,* when our talks went from trivial to substantial. We started talking about her songwriting and her moving to Atlanta to pursue her career. Later it was going to hair school. Until I asked the question, "Do you have a plan?"

Impact or change can often start with one simple question. A probing question, that evokes thought and asks, "How can I help you go from where you are, to where you want to be?" From there, we began a coaching relationship. We talked once a week and reviewed options. I made some suggestions, we did some job hunting exercises, and at the time, it was clear that Samia did not want to be a hairdresser. A lyrical soul, creativity and ideas flow from her with ease. It was during those initial coaching sessions that I first heard the word *Gurlification.* It was an idea that Samia had for T-shirts. In the original idea, *Gurlification* would go on the front of the T-shirt, and a rule for being a young lady on the back.

It sounded cute, simple and easy, I encouraged Samia to pursue it. *Gurlification* could become another stream of income, and possibly jumpstart her career as a singer/songwriter. She could use the money from the T-shirts to pay for studio time or create a mix tape. Breaking into the music industry is much different today than in years past. Time passed, and she stopped calling, I never said much when I went to get my hair done. Occasionally, she'd mention not going to Atlanta or hair school, but that was pretty much it. Samia had started "washing her nets."

*"So it was, as the multitude pressed about Him to hear the word of God, that He stood by the Lake of Gennesaret, and saw two boats standing by the lake; but the fishermen had gone from them and were washing their nets," Luke 5:1-2.* The fishermen had given up! They had fished all night and caught nothing. They tried every possible thing they could to catch something, anything; but they caught nothing. We've all been there, stuck between the mundane and mediocre. What do you do when you don't know what to do? You wash your nets. Washing your nets is not necessarily giving up, but it can also be realizing that you have done all you can do. You have exhausted all of your resources and there is nothing left to do; so you wash your nets, and call it a day.

*Don't Be Afraid of the Silence*

I love to talk. But, my coach training taught me that I had to learn to listen. Not just listen, but I had to learn not to be afraid of the silence. It's so easy to interrupt someone when they're talking by injecting a comment. It's easy to strike up a conversation, engage the other person, or push them to answer a question. I have learned over the years, not to be afraid of the silence. By not being afraid of the silence, you are not only listening to what the person is saying, but what they are not saying. If Samia didn't want to talk about her future plans, neither did I. But what I realized during those silent years, yes years, was that she didn't need a coach, she needed a mentor. She needed someone to pour into her first; spiritually and then personally and professionally. Pouring into someone requires the mentor to be transparent. She's seen me at my best and my worst. Change is hard for all of us. The reason change is hard is because deep down we really don't want to deny ourselves. We don't want to exchange our will for God's but think that we can keep doing what we want to do and please God at the same time. News flash, it doesn't work that way, you can't please God and yourself. Even though change is hard, it's necessary if you're going to fulfill purpose. So while I was in coaching mode, using all the tools and expertise; it was mentoring and watering time.

I have developed somewhat of a reputation as a stalker from my mentees, but we weren't' there yet, so it was silent, and I wasn't afraid of it. I just let it play out, not knowing God had a plan for the both of us.

*Designing Hope*

I had my book signing for *Drop Your Baggage* at The Cheltenham Square Mall. The book signing was part of what became an annual event called, *Makeover Madness*. It was part of *Breast Cancer Awareness Month*.

The Mall gave three deserving contestants total makeovers from head to toe speakers, vendors, and activities, ending with the contestants' presentations. It was so empowering!

## The Power of One

The winners were awarded free coaching and kept outfits provided by shops such as, Burlington Coat Factory, and Ashley Stewart. I was so inspired; I began thinking about a reality show or docu-series. This show would center on a young lady, following her, coaching her, and providing resources on her journey from low-income housing to home-ownership. The show was to be called *Designing Hope*. I shot a trailer with a young lady by the name of Christine Lightford, which included a session with a housing counselor. I never really pitched it to producers. However, in the end it was worth it. Christine got her house, and I was glad to be part of it. The show was to be called *Designing Hope*.

Reality television has taken such a bad rap. You have to take the good with the bad. We rave about *Scandal* and *Revenge,* but criticize the *Real Housewives* series. Don't get me wrong, some of it is ridiculous and insulting, but it is what it is. However, for every *Real Housewives* there's *Six Little McGhees* or *Welcome to Sweetie Pie*'s.

I saw *Designing Hope* as a chance to impact lives by sharing stories of transformation and transition. I wasn't trying to be Iyanla; I only wanted to bring to the screen the things I'd already been doing on a daily basis.

While talking about Designing Hope to my friend Shari Williams, Shari also had an idea about a show. I decided to call Rachelle Ricks of Philly Girl Productions. After a few meetings and catching up, she thought the real story was Kay and I. Now here was a perfect combination of tension, love and turmoil. The connection Kay and I shared, good and bad, was undeniable. It would have burst off the screen!

Unfortunately, Kay decided she didn't want to do it. Vulnerability and transparency can be a lot to ask of some people. While it has never been a struggle for me, I'm an open book.

Rachelle was persistent, "There are girls like Kay everywhere, and you know how to reach and help them, let's keep it moving," she said.

If I have learned nothing else about mentoring, it is that in order to have an impact, there must be a genuine, authentic connection.

You can't fake it! Regardless of the situation, or circumstances, if there's no connection, there's no change. No change, no impact. I was sitting on the edge of my bed, thinking about the show, the-who, the-where, and the-why. As I got out of my bed I began to pray and ask God who. His response was clear, Samia. I got excited thinking about Samia because of her musical aspirations. I know so many musicians and producers.

I could shoot an episode with my friend Grammy-nominated producer Anthony Bell, who has worked with Jill Scott, Common, Jewel, and Luke James, But I also thought about *Gurlification*.

I asked Naneke, her reply was, "I think she would be perfect."

Forget what you see on television, there is nothing easy about doing a documentary, or a television reality show.

It takes work and most importantly, money; because of the time it consumes, a shoestring budget really doesn't work. I've done short films on "zero." But for television, shoestring doesn't really work because of the various dynamics and intricacies involved. We pushed on anyway. Rachelle met Samia, liked her immediately. So we moved forward.

*The Covenant*

Since Samia and I were not necessarily picking up from where we left off, I started with the covenant. A covenant is a solemn agreement between you and another party to join in harmony with the precepts of the gospel of Jesus Christ. The covenant outlined action steps and assignments that we both agreed on.

Once I heard Bishop Charles Mellette say, "A covenant relationship is a relationship commitment arranged by God, necessary for us to carry out our creative purpose."

If we chose our relationships, we would choose them based solely on our best interest. If it were left to us, we'd choose our own siblings, our own bosses, friends, and co-workers. Fortunately for us, God didn't leave certain relationships up to us, knowing that we would dismiss people who we needed in our lives as contributors to our growth and development. We need each other to fulfill purpose so that we may mature and grow together.

There is not one person whom I have mentored whom I chose, not one. God sent them, he positioned me, and he ordained the relationship. Samia's covenant had three action steps: spiritual growth, financial responsibility (tithing, savings, spending plan) and a business plan.

As a serial entrepreneur, I love working with start-ups. The covenant was written into the show.

However, God had another plan, and it was just as Bishop Mellette described, a covenant relationship necessary for Samia and I, to carry out our creative purpose.

*There's Rules to This.*

*Designing Hope* slowly began to take a back seat, as it became increasingly clear that there were not enough resources to videotape our everyday lives. There were too many missed opportunities.

While Samia loved music, our focus became *Gurlification*. As we moved through the process of writing the business plan, registering the business, and preparing for the launch, I felt more and more a part of the process. The birthing of *Gurlification* was a lot different than the process of starting Michele Thomas's (*With This Ring Wedding Chapel), another business I helped to launch.* The same holds true with Jennifer Adams on her salon launch called *Salon of Salons* or even Naneke opening *The Beauty Studio*.

We were growing together and *Gurlification* was the vehicle. It was my assignment to push Samia toward a closer relationship with the Lord first, and He in turn would reveal her destiny. Unfortunately, *God's ways truly are not our ways, nor are His thoughts our thoughts (Isaiah 55:8).*

## The Power of One

I was just going with the flow, certain that after the launch, I would move on as I always do. However, somewhere during the business planning, designing the line and planning the launch, Samia asked, "Can we be business partners?" I had never considered it. I'm an evangelist. Get in, and get out. I believed in *Gurlification*, what it represented. I also believe there are rules of etiquette when becoming a young lady, and getting that message out is necessary now more than ever. More importantly, I believed in Samia. I believed in her gifts, her talents, and her dreams. Eventually, as we shared our lives, God would use us to make a difference in the lives of young girls, teenagers and other young women. *Gurlification* was about more than T-shirts. Samia's vision was to have a store with everything for girls; makeup, feminine hygiene products, lingerie, hair care and etiquette classes. *Gurlification* could eventually become a social enterprise, a company that would not only make money but make a difference.

There were times however when I felt like we were on opposite ends of the earth. I'd go left Samia would go right. We were not clicking, not building, the connection was challenging. I'd call Naneke complaining and asking questions on how to get Samia to open up to me. As a mentor you have expectations, some are unrealistic at times. It can be frustrating when a person you're trying to help doesn't always make decisions you'd like them to make, or not moving and growing at the pace you think they should. However, a covenant relationship means you do not give up on the person by quitting or throwing in the towel. You can throw up your hands, but don't throw in the towel!

## Tanya T. Morris

It was still early in the process, when my friend Mister Mann Frisby posted a flyer for the grand opening of Impact Boutique on Facebook. I reached out and asked him about the owner Caron Nikole. An amazing person; Caron had her MBA before she was 30, a lifetime of experience personally and professionally. I asked Mister to see if Caron would be interested in mentoring Samia.

We went to the grand opening, they clicked and Samia began volunteering at Impact on her days off.

Mentorship extends beyond the one on one.

I'm always looking for opportunities and resources for my protégés. I don't know everything, but if I don't know, I'll do everything I can to find out. Caron could give Samia so much more than I ever could about retail, wholesale, and fashion design. I also reached out to my friend of 10 plus years Hakim Harrell who directed us to industry trade shows, and printed our first T-shirts. We met with Jabir Rahman, owner of Pimp My Tees, who created a million-dollar clothing line in his home. He did our first prototypes and continues to share his knowledge and experience. The official launch party was beyond successful! Yet in the back of my mind I was still thinking my partnership would be temporary. My goal was to put Samia in position to do *Gurlification* full-time, put all the systems in place and move on. But it just didn't happen!

I never saw myself running a T-shirt business but it was fun. The events, the people, and the fashion industry are not my area, but I love small business and marketing. *Gurlification* had given me the opportunity to bridge my talents and passion for mentoring together all at once.

Since we started, *Gurlification* has been featured in the *Philadelphia Tribune,* the *Philadelphia Daily News,* online, and in stores. It's being worn by recording artist, radio personalities and around the way girls.

As I said earlier, there is a lesson in every mentoring relationship. As time passed and Gurlification grew, I locked in for the long haul. We were accepted into *Elevate*, a 12-month growth program for 'early stage' businesses at The Enterprise Center, which provides access to capital, capacity building, business education and economic development opportunities to minority entrepreneurs.

It was the first day of class and the guest speaker was Della Clark, the Executive Director. I've met her before but today was different. Today she shared with us the keys to business success and my greatest takeaway was "know your numbers." Knowing your numbers means that you know why you do what you do, how you do it and if it's working. But also have to know where what you do is taking you. That's something only the numbers can show you. Originally from Texas, Clark has been an important part of The Enterprise Center in West Philadelphia for 23 years.

Della Clark has presence!

It's not physical; it's her confidence and assurance that shines through in her speech and her approach. She makes an impact and believes given the resources and opportunity; minority businesses can make an impact.

That's why she remains steadfast in her mission to help minority businesses grow.

Under her leadership TEC runs Community Leaders a nine-month training program. It gave a home to culinary entrepreneurs in 2008 when it opened the Dorrance H. Hamilton Culinary Center. And in 2010, TEC launched the **Walnut Hill Community Farm**, a youth-based urban agriculture initiative and partnered with Urban Tree Connection to administer a youth-run Community Supported Agriculture program West Philly Foods. Hundreds, possibly thousands of businesses have come through The Enterprise Center. "This is my assignment in life. I feel I don't need to be recognized because I enjoy the work so much."

When you love what you do, and keep doing it with same veracity everyday, and don't need to be recognized that's power that makes an impact and changes lives. And that first day I knew *Elevate* was going to make a major impact on both of our lives.

*Elevate* was a great learning opportunity for us. It was a chance to create a strategic plan that would guide us on the journey toward Samia's exit from the *Beauty Studio*, to *Gurlification* full-time.

However, somewhere between events and Elevate Samia started to question if *Gurlification* was what she wanted to do. I had my own doubts. Every other month I'd say, "This was the last thing I was going to do" whatever that thing was. But like the mob, every time I thought I was out, the chase for success pulled me back in! Life is funny that way. You can think you're on the right path and headed in the right direction, or at least doing your best, but sometimes your best doesn't make you happy nor does it satisfy. We've all been there, where what we are doing doesn't satisfy. I once heard Ukee Washington, a local Philadelphia newscaster say, "If you love what you do, you will never work a day in your life"! That's satisfaction.

Whatever it was I could see that Samia was not engaged. As much as I didn't want to admit it, I was beyond disappointed; this was her thing? When we eventually talked about what was next for *Gurlification*, I realized what I was supposed to learn from this latest mentoring journey; how to separate business relationships from personal relationships. This was the first time a mentoring relationship became a business partnership, and those are two very different relationships. I could never see *Gurlification* without Samia nor did I want to.

I had to realize that for all the times I said to her, "*Gurlification* isn't about you," I kept making it about her, for that reason I kept it going. I continued doing events, tweeting and posting about *Gurlificaiton*.

Disappointment was continually brewing inside of me. I wanted to scream, sometimes I cried but I pressed my way through it.

The natural order of life is that there will always be seed time and harvest. When you plant and sow a seed, it is supposed to bare fruit. For all the money, time, and talents that were invested, I was still waiting for the seed to grow, waiting for it to bloom into this beautiful business. Rain in the form of tears only matters to those who have a seed in the ground. To everyone else it's a nuisance. I expected fruit! Whether it was the business growing, or Samia growing, there was a seed in the ground and it had to produce. I was going to quit *Elevate*. I felt like I had done enough small business classes. When I contacted the program, Gabrielle, the coordinator, would hear none of it! She gave me assignments and insisted I see them through, so I did.

It was at our holiday gathering with classmates that the idea of doing an event first came up. The idea was, *"Look Pretty, Think Pretty Day,"* which was one of *Gurlification's* rules. I mulled it over during the holiday.

I met *Miss Teen Pennsylvania* at State Senator Vincent Hughes' holiday party, and planned to stay in touch. When the New Year came in, I asked her to co-host. I sent the date to Iola Harper, Program Director at the Enterprise Center and she said how about calling it *"Pretty in the City."*

Never underestimate small or what sometimes may be considered trivial conversations. It's small conversations over dinner with friends where some of our best ideas are birthed. So, I put the wheels in motion. I asked Miss *Teen Pennsylvania Jasmine Daniels,* to host along with recording artist Bria Marie. I put together a fashion show with girls from the *Achieving Independence Center*, a program for foster-care youth. I arranged press events, and a social media campaign, I was so excited!

About two weeks prior to the event Samia called and asked if I needed any help. We talked several times leading up to the event, bringing her up to date on the

## The Power of One

details. One of the things I always aim for in mentoring is consistency. I never asked why or got into the what's with Samia, we just went to work. I trusted she would figure things out in her own time. Through it all, we are a great team! The event was excellent; it really showed the value, the fun and character of *Gurlification* as a movement. It was in many ways a new beginning for us. We now host and coordinate our own special events including fashion shows, girls' night out, slumber parties and networking events.

We completed *Elevate* together. Since then we've launched a new website and our events calendar is full. We will also be launching a line for girls' ages 8 to12. Our approach is a little different than it was when we started. However, our goal is to build a lifestyle brand synonymous with women and style that inspires both the young and old to be ladylike.

We all grow and change in our own time. Although Samia was not the first person I mentored, she is the one I am the most invested. Our relationship still fluctuates between mentor-protégé, mother-daughter, business partners, teacher-student or her favorite girlfriends.

She thinks I go to far drawing the line of girlfriends but I'm not your girlfriend, and you are not my peer. Basically our relationship exists in phases or levels it's provincial. Sometimes we all need another mother, another voice who challenges our thinking and lovingly corrects us. Mentorship is designed to pull out of the protégé talents and abilities that will take them further than the mentor or protégé could ever imagine.

The right combination of love and correction makes mentoring like any other friendship, whereby you frequently ask how did I get into this and how can I get out of it! Once I told Rachel that of all the ladies I have mentored, Samia is the one I am the most proud of. I meant it then and I mean it even more now.

## Impact Activity.
*The Mentorship Circle*

Mentorship is typically done one-on-one. However mentoring can also be a series of relationships or conversations designed to take you from where you are to where you want to be. Create your mentorship circle by assessing your needs and record, and list the people who meet the need and help turn your goal into an accomplishment.

# TEN

## Leadership
## AGENTS OF S.H.I.E.L.D.

### **AGENTS OF S.H.I.E.L.D.**
*(Selfless, Humble, Intelligent, Empathetic, Logical and Determined.)*

# The Power of One

**M**arvel Comics defines AGENTS OF S.H.I.E.L.D. as an elite team of agents who investigate strange occurrences around the globe, and protect regular citizens from the extraordinary. Each brings a specialty to the group.

The following are my AGENTS OF S.H.I.E.L.D. and each of them bring something different to the table, each have their own super power. They do share some general characteristics that you should be able to identify within your inner circle or at least seek out as you assemble your own AGENTS.

Leadership is the most authentic demonstration of the power of one. It is the ability to be heard without being seen, it is advocating, standing up and coming through in an instant. In 2014, I enrolled in the *Executive Leadership MBA Program* at Strayer University. I have pursued a master's degree more than once, been in at least two programs. I am still irritated that I wasn't accepted to the University of Pennsylvania especially since I had 30 MBA credits at the time I applied. Nevertheless, Strayer University has proven to be the right program, and the best decision I have ever made. I never expected to be getting my MBA at 50, but here I am. It's funny how we never know how much we want something until it's close enough for us to touch it. That's how I feel about the MBA I never knew I wanted it until I actually saw and knew that I was going to get it!

When I started the program at Strayer, the first class required a **DISC** Management Assessment and Leadership Profile.

I am a DI, (Dominant and Influence) the two strong characteristics of any leader who is going to make a difference. Dominant doesn't mean that you have to always be in charge or in control. Dominant is certainty of your role and embracing it.

The greatest responsibility of any leader is people development. Jack Welch, former CEO of General Electric, who is credited with its turnaround, said "People development is a daily event, integrated into every aspect of your regular goings-on." There is no greater joy than seeing people develop and fulfill their purpose and destiny. Leadership is people development personified. It is the epitome of The *Power of One*. Leadership, and particularly leadership development, is paramount in the Christian church. Unfortunately, some leaders have lost sight of the goal to make disciples. Making disciples requires leading by example.

However, regardless of the vocation leadership is a great responsibility. In the words of Ben Parker, Peter Parker AKA Spider-Man's uncle, "With great power, comes great responsibility."

# ELEVEN
# The Advocate

*Everybody needs someone to speak for them when they can't speak for themselves.*

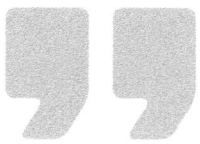

The Power of One

**To this date Jean Hunt remains one of my favorite supervisors.** She's been retired for five years or so, but that hasn't changed my occasional phone call for counsel or a reference. She's always available. She's not just one of my favorite bosses; she's easily one of my favorite people. Jean's super power is advocacy. I often tell young people to mark the person who changes the way you view the world. That's an AGENT!

When I met Jean, I was working for *W.A.W.A.* now it's *PathWays PA*. She had just come on board as the Executive Director of the *Campaign for Working Families* when I started as the community outreach coordinator at *PathWays PA*, a campaign partner. While that was the start of my outreach career, Jean's began protesting the Vietnam War in 1965.

The formation of this program was without a doubt one of my most enjoyable experiences. Watching all of these different organizations; *the Greater Philadelphia Urban Affairs Coalition; The United Way; the IRS; The Reinvestment Fund*, and countless of others bringing their talents, their time, money and resources together to help working families move up the economic ladder was most enjoyable. It started at the *Fox Leadership Center*, at the *University of Pennsylvania*, and later moved to the offices of the *Urban Affairs Coalition* in July 2003. UAC has served as its managing partner ever since. Supported by a strong group of local partners, the Campaign for Working Families provides free tax services, access to savings products, credit counseling, financial education, information about public benefits, and other programs and services in neighborhoods throughout Philadelphia.

To date the Campaign has filed over 145,000 returns. Brought $236 million in tax refund, saved families in interest fees and charges for tax preparation, check cashing, and loans $28 million. But for Jean it wasn't just about the numbers. It was about the economic power it gave families.

A community organizer in the '60s and '70s, Jean worked on civil rights, anti-war and women's issues. A registered nurse for twenty years, she was recruited to work at the City of Philadelphia Department of Parks and Recreation in 1994.

Jean's job was to raise money for neighborhoods supporting to expand programming.

During her tenure they expanded sports programs for girls, organized soccer for 40,000 of Philadelphian' children, created an environmental educational summer camp and after school program.

Later, Jean became the *Directory of Children, Youth and Families Programs at the William Penn Foundation* before leading the Campaign from 2003 to 2010.

## The Power of One

*"We created a powerful, citywide network of people committed to a common purpose: assisting low-income working families in order to help them improve their economic situation,"* Jean said.

It was the collaboration between neighborhood leaders, churches, law firms, businesses, government, colleges and universities.

It was real advocacy, real power in one voice because we were able to articulate the issues involved in predatory services clearly.

We were good at educating people about the perils of predatory lending, and our work was so widely respected, that we were part of a national effort *(National Community Tax Coalition)* that was able to save the *Earned Income Tax Credit* several years in a row from drastic cuts urged by the House of Representatives. We did this through advocacy. Whether it was knocking on doors, getting petitions signed, congressional visits in Harrisburg or sit-ins at H&R Block, we would not be moved.

*"We were effective at organizing and outreach, and we were able to help large numbers of families save the money they would have spent on commercial tax preparers and check cashing stores."* Jean said.

*"Low and moderate income people need to be able to control the money they do have and protect it from a market that seeks to strip them of their resources,"* Jean said when I caught up with her while she was babysitting her grandchildren.

## Tanya T. Morris

The commercial marketplace is full of products and services that generate huge profits from bad products that rip off low wageworkers. Efforts like the Campaign, help people to understand ways they can take control of their own households, make their own best decisions about how their bills get paid, and how their money gets used.

It's through advocacy and education people learn they are not alone, they also learn their financial issues are not a personal problem, but rather a structural problem with the economic system. Advocacy begins with organizing, good organizing, and bringing people together in a common effort in a way that helps them feel their own strength, articulating a problem in a clear and understandable fashion, and then, together devising a strategy for change that people agree with and will fight to implement.

Jean was the first person I knew who tipped the housekeeping staff during a hotel stay. I'm ashamed to say I never thought about it.

"You leave a tip in the room," I asked. "Yes. Do you know how much a housekeeper makes?"

I was clueless. It was during my time at The Campaign that I read *The Working Poor: Invisible in America* by David K. Shipler and *Nickel and Dimed* by Barbara Ehrenreich, both books changed the way I viewed the disproportion of wealth in America.

It wasn't until Barack Obama became President, did our nation even come remotely close to universal health care. But it has been an everyday way of life in Canada for over a decade. Recently there's been a push to increase the minimum wage, arguments that it's not a living wage. Well, Jean and former *WAWA Executive* Director Carol Goertzel were talking about and advocating for a living wage 15 to 20 years ago. You may not see the outcomes from your advocacy and organizing efforts, some things take a little more time to produce desired results. Eventually, it will yield results even if it's on a small scale. Ultimately, the hope is that these efforts can lead to the creation of a fairer marketplace.

*Activate Your Advocacy Super Power*

Growing up one of my favorite cartoons was *The Super Friends*. I don't what today's cartoons are about. A sponge that talks? Anyway, back in the day there was always a moral to the story or a message. When The Wonder Twins joined *The Super Friends* I thought they were corny. They were different from the other Super Friends because their super powers were activated when they touched each other. "Wonder Twin Powers, activate!" Once they touched, each would announce their intended form. Zac could transform into water at any state (solid, liquid, gas) Jayna could transform into any animal; whether real, mythological, and indigenous to Earth or to some other planet. Here's another cool thing, when one was in trouble, each could alert the other over a distance telepathically. Imagine if you were in danger, needed help with a problem or someone to go to bat for you; being able to signal or alert an advocate. Not just anyone, but the person you know will advocate, stand in the gap and make a real difference in your life. Advocacy is passion, and to advocate for change, and be an agent, you must have passion.

What are you passionate about? I was on my way to have an oil change and the car in front of me had an SPCA emblem, 'I'm an advocate for animals' bumper sticker.

Everybody is passionate about something! Whales, dogs, homelessness, gay rights, and the environment you name it.

Advocacy is public support for a recommendation of a particular case or policy. Without organizing, planning, and passion it's just noise, being the loudest person in the room but never going out and taking action won't produce anything. You can never make an impact without action.

In the familiar story of David and Goliath, David went to the battlefield to take his brothers lunch. When he got there he heard the taunts of Goliath. He wasn't just shouting or making threats, he was in David's words, "defying the army of the living God." When David's brothers asked why he was there and accused him of being nosy. David calmly replied, "What have I done, Is there not a cause?" David was asking isn't there a reason, a purpose? Isn't God worth standing up and fighting for? What is the cause? What is the reason that is worth fighting for that requires passion, education and organizing to change your life and the lives of those connected to you? Find it and go make a difference.

## TWELVE

# The Frankford Fighter

*We're mad as hell, and we're not going to take it anymore!"* Howard Beale

## The Power of One

One of the first people I met when I started working for Turning Points was Kim Washington, Executive Director of the Frankford Community Development Corporation. I needed to establish some strong community partners and the CDC was the best place to start. After law school Kim returned to her roots in Frankford first as the Equal Partners in Change Coordinator.

EPIC was a community engagement group; funded by the Department of Human Services to address quality of life issues in the Lower Northeast through prevention based programing.

In 2011, Kim developed a small private practice; where she served as attorney for children and families involved in the Philadelphia child welfare system and families involved in child custody and support matters. Kim is a passionate, driven fighter for the community she grew up in and loves. Under her leadership as the *Executive Director for the Frankford Community Development Corporation,* the CDC provides residents with affordable housing resources, employment, and entrepreneurial opportunities.

It manages the Frankford Avenue Commercial Corridor. Frankford Ave. has a rich tradition of shopping. Not a day passes when I don't hear someone say how it's changed and how he or she remembers coming down to the avenue to shop. Kim's super power is strategic planning. If you are truly going to make an impact you must have a strategy. All too often we just go through life by the seat of our pants. Some call it freedom. The reality is that every area of your life requires a strategy. Strategy is a carefully outlined plan that combines methods with directives. This super power is one that not only transforms but also stabilizes. Unfortunately, for many inner city neighborhoods, gentrification has become all too common and Frankford is no exception.

There are various opinions as to the intention and goal of gentrification; but at the end of the day it comes down to money.

> *"People seem to have a hard time figuring out how to create neighborhoods that are economically and racially diverse,"* Washington said.

Gentrification is the easy way to transform a neighborhood. Once a neighborhood is seen as blighted and property values drop low enough, it creates a ripe opportunity for an investor to come in at a low price and develop the neighborhood for a wealthier population of individuals who will give the developer the highest return on their investment." This puts residents who live in that community, who lack the wealth, or who don't own their home, at a disadvantage. Basically it pushes them out. This is one of the things that I admire and appreciate most about Frankford. The residents there are lifers and they are as invested now, as they were twenty, thirty years ago. As most know once a neighborhood starts to gentrify it's hard to try and slow it down. The key is to stabilize a neighborhood long before it becomes in such disrepair that it's ripe for investors to come in and make a profit off the neighborhood. The *Frankford Transportation Center* is the second busiest station on Philadelphia's public transportation city railways. Nearly twenty thousand people pass through it daily. Kim's strategic planning power has been on display recently as she wages war against the *Southeastern Pennsylvania Transportation Authority (SEPTA)*; to be a community partner, and economic developer on three parcels of land at the terminal.

> *"Any effort to "transform a neighborhood" without providing economic development (job creation, quality retail services, and quality affordable housing) first, will only result in gentrification,"* she said.

After being frustrated for months, meeting after meeting with SEPTA officials and no resolve, Kim took the fight to them. In less than two days she strategized and pulled together thirty-five residents to openly protest a SEPTA board meeting. A printer on the avenue printed T-shirts, transportation was provided by local churches, the CDC provided lunch and water. As a community partner I organized the media. The meeting started and ended with Kim's Network inspired, *"We're mad as hell, and we're not going to take it anymore!"* speech.

You see, SEPTA had made promises dating back twenty years and hadn't delivered, all the while businesses on the avenue suffered. The meeting was over in thirty minutes. Since then Kim has continued to strategize, sacrificing sleep and any plans for a summer vacation.

She has worked tirelessly with *the Philadelphia Planning Commission,* political officials and the community to ensure that real economic development comes to Frankford.

*"We just want something more, something that the community needs, something that could spur additional development and provide jobs,"* Washington said, all the while strategizing her next steps.

# THIRTEEN
# A Leader's Leader

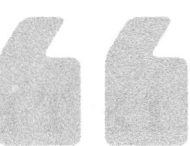

"This lesser world is all about reproduction, as you might well know. Those who cease to duplicate simply die." RawiHage, Carnival: A Novel

## The Power of One

**I**f you have read one of my other books you've probably heard me talk about **Bishop James Darrell Robinson, Sr.** I quote him, I reference his stories and testimonies. Bishop Darrell has been preaching since he was 14 and he's been in ministry for over 30 years. Bishop Robinson is a leader's leader. His super power is duplication. The best way to measure the impact of leadership is his/her ability to develop and reproduce other leaders.

I met Bishop Robinson in 1994 at *East Coast Express*, an entertainment management and promotions company. He was also pastor of the Philadelphia Revival Temple.

I remember the first time we met; the first time I visited his church. But my greatest memory is a conversation we had one night on a ride home after Bible Study. I knew there was a calling on my life; remember my grandmother had been telling me that since I was a child. Sometimes you may know your life has purpose and meaning, but need someone to direct you and steer you in the right direction by making sure you get the tools and right information you need so you don't forfeit or abort your purpose. That night, Bishop Robinson revealed he was the man for the job. I was always asking questions about the word, about ministry.

This time Bishop calmly answered, "It's obvious there's a calling on your life, he said. "Just keep coming to Bible study, coming on Sundays, and I'm going to mentor you and help you develop character first."

From then until now, everything I know about leadership and ministry I learned from James Darrell Robinson.

Bishop isn't just a pastor, apostle and overseer, but a concert promoter, producer, husband, father, musician, activist, and philanthropist. I could go on and on talking about his real estate and computer programing expertise, but that would just be overkill. Another one of his attributes is resilience. Resilience is the ability to bounce back. When his mother was diagnosed with Alzheimer's, he became her primary caregiver. He didn't rush to put her in a nursing home; no instead he took her with him to every meeting, every event and every service. Strong character and resilience are things that every leader must have if he's going to be effective in producing other leaders.

There's always this great debate about whether leaders are born or made. I believe leadership is a skill, and therefore leaders can be developed. There are characteristics leaders possess that are inherent.

However, character and leadership skills must be developed. Character is built and shaped through our experiences, upbringing, trials and tribulations. One of my favorite Bishop Robinson sayings came from one of his teachers who used to say, *"Darrell, have character, don't be one."* That always stuck with me because there are always opportunities to act out of character.

Situations and circumstances can often cause the most consistent person to behave in a way they are not accustomed.

Resourcefulness is another one of Bishop's attributes. A resourceful leader is a powerful leader. Being resourceful doesn't mean you have to know everything.

When you're resourceful, it means that if you don't have the answer, you know where to get it. Being resourceful is about relationships. One that says because you have maintained good relationships at work, communities, places of worship, friends that you can always go to can tap that resource when needed. Being resourceful means that you have built long-lasting relationships. One thing I am not afraid of is picking up the phone. All you can do is ask, but what to do with the yes or the no is something you learn to work out and strategize.

One thing that Bishop would always say to us in leadership class is that he wants us not only to learn what to do as a leader, but also what not to do. He consistently strived for balance. Maintaining balance in your approach is essential to duplication.

I always strive for consistency, and trust me it is not easy. There were times I wanted to walk away from my responsibilities at work, home, and in ministry. There were times when I wanted to go off, and there were times when I wanted to lock myself away from everyone, I couldn't because I knew at the end of the day nothing would be gained and I would not be better. When looking at leadership and mentorship, duplication asks the question, did the mentee and/or follower go further than the mentor or leader? I want to see Samia, Nakia and even Kay, go further than me, personally, professionally, spiritually and in their relationships. Bishop Robinson may never write a book, but I have written three. I have started several businesses.

*Gurlification* continues to grow even with all its ups and downs. Just as others, and I can see Bishop Robinson in me, I want to be able to see myself in those that I mentor. Duplication isn't just accomplishments or traveling the world. Duplication starts with character. Do you have the characteristics and attributes that lead to success and achievement by tapping into the power of one so you can go and make an impact?

# FOURTEEN

# The Mother of Reinvention

## The Power of One

**In January 2013 I hosted my first goal party.** Every year after Christmas, the world begins making New Year resolutions. Weight loss, exercising, savings, going back to school, etc. However, after celebrating the New Year, shifting gears from a holiday mindset to work mindset, resolutions are soon forgotten by the time the rat race called life kicks in. What is often overlooked is that a resolution is a formal expression of intention. It is a decision or a determination.

A resolution is an intention; it doesn't require responsibility to take action because it's just intent. There's an old saying "the road to hell is paved with good intentions". And that's where it falls apart for most of us—we honestly never intended to take action or make those changes. It just sounded good at the time and since everybody else was doing it, we figured I better do something also. I created the goal party because the New Year is a new beginning and another opportunity to do something great.

The new beginning, and new opportunity begins with goals. So many of us go into the New Year with no plan, no goals, no anything, because we have settled with being average. If you do not have a plan for your life, for your family, for your relationships or for your spiritual development then you have settled for average. Goals mean that you are taking responsibility for completing the task, for finishing. It requires action and a goal without a plan is just a wish.

I have spent the majority of my professional career in nonprofit sector. My career has been filled with ups and downs. The nonprofit sector is so unpredictable especially for smaller organizations. Nonprofit can be very fulfilling but very frustrating at the same time. By working for nonprofit organizations I have had to recreate myself more times than I choose to remember. Even while temping, I worked at nonprofits doing some menial task, mostly administration. But each one of those assignments, with a degree, gave me an experience or a skill that I could use later in my professional career.

In order to truly change your life you have to be flexible and adaptable. My first job out of college was a reporter, never, ever wanted to be a newspaper reporter, but the discipline I needed to diversify my writing could never have been learned in a better place than the newsroom at the *Philadelphia Daily News, Philadelphia Sunday Sun* and *Philadelphia Tribune*. There were times when I read the edits and thought, "I don't remember writing that." Other times, the changes were so drastic, I didn't recognize the story and wanted to fight my editor!

When I moved on to the Kintock Group I did little or no writing until the conversation with a resident named Vernon Rouse inspired my first book. When I went to WAWA later the Women's Opportunities Resource Center, the Campaign, Consumer Credit Counseling,

ECA and Turning Points after that, I reinvented myself each and every time so that I could be effective and have an impact on those I served.

The apostle Paul put it this way, *"to the weak I became as weak, that I might win the weak. I have become all things to all men that I might by all means save some."* (1Cor 9:22)

Reinventing yourself is adapting to what the person or situation requires to not only win them over, but also to save yourself from yourself. Becoming weak is to be vulnerable and empathetic to the circumstances others find themselves in, a way that allows you to open yourself up to change. Change your life and you will inevitably change others.

# Bonus Chapter
# Resources and More!

Throughout The Power of One I have shared stories of people, organizations, resources and processes that I use to make a difference. As a bonus here are some organizations and resources that I use and refer to my family, friends and clients. Some service Philadelphia region but others are national. If they can't service you check your area for similar resources and organizations and go make an impact!

**PathwaysPA (formerly Women's Assoc. for Women's Alternatives)**
310 Amosland Road
Holmes, PA 19043
P 610-543-5022 | F 610-543-1549
www.pathwayspa.org

**Benjamin's Desk**
1701 Walnut St.
Philadelphia, PA 19103
P: 267-765-2070
www.benjaminsdesk.com

**OIC**
1231 North Broad St
Philadelphia, PA 19122
P: 215-236-7700
www.philaoic.org

**A&R Personal Assistance**
P: 215-479-1942 | F: 215-533-8589
www.ARPAservices.com

**Entrepreneur Works**
111 S Independence Mall E #528
Philadelphia, PA 19106
215-543-3100
www.myentrepreneurworks.org

**The Campaign for Working Families**
1415 N. Broad St. Suite 221-A
Philadelphia, PA 19122
P 215-454-6483 | F 267-457-2655
www.cwfphilly.org

**Urban Affairs Coalition**
1207 Chestnut Street
Philadelphia, PA 19107
P 215-851-0110 | F 215-851-0514
www.uac.org

**Clarifi (formerly Consumer Credit Counseling Services of the Delaware Valley)**
1608 Walnut Street, 10th Floor
Philadelphia, PA 19103
P: 215-563-5665 | F: 215-563-7020
www.clarifi.org

**Turning Points for Children**
415 S. 15th Street
Philadelphia, PA 19146
P: 215.875.8200 | E: info@tp4c.org
www.turningpointsforchildren.org

**Public Citizens for Children and Youth**
1709 Benjamin Franklin Pkwy
Philadelphia, PA 19103
P: 215-563-0677
www.pccy.org

**Yesha Ministries Worship Center**
2301 Snyder Ave.
Philadelphia, PA 19145
P 215-271-4017
www.yeshaministries.org

**The Beauty Studio**
400 W. Chelten Ave.
Philadelphia, PA 19144
P 215-848-6880
thebeautystudio@comcast.net

**Gurlification**
www.gurlification.com

**IMPACT HUB**
394 Broadway, 5th Floor
New York, NY 10013
P: 212-880-9767
www.impacthubnyc.com

**The Energy Coordinating Agency**
106 W. Clearfield St.
Philadelphia, PA 19133
P 215-609-1000 | F 215-988-0919
www.ecasavesenergy.org

**Philadelphia Corporation for Aging**
642 N Broad St.
Philadelphia, PA 19130
215-765-9040
www.pcacares.org

**American Heart Association**
1617 John F Kennedy Blvd # 700
Philadelphia, PA 19103
P 215-575-5200
www.heart.org/philadelphia

**Mothers In Charge**
The Riverview Place
520 N. Delaware Ave, Suite 302
Philadelphia, PA 19123
www.mothersincharge.org

**Frankford Community Development Corporation**
4900 Griscom Street
Philadelphia, PA 19124
P 215-743-6580 | F 215-743-6582

**Women's Opportunities Resource Center (WORC)**
2010 Chestnut St.
Philadelphia, PA 19100
P 215-564-5500 | F 215-564-0933
www.worc-pa.com

**The Enterprise Center**
4548 Market St.
Philadelphia, PA 19139
215-895-4000
www.theenterprisecenter.com

**Sustainable Business Network of Philadelphia**
2401 Walnut Street, Suite 206
Philadelphia, PA 19103
P 215-922-7400 | 267-233-1778
info@sbnphiladelphia.org

**Finanta**
1301 N Second Street
Philadelphia, PA 19122
P 267 236-7025 | F 267 236-7008
www.finanta.org

**The Urban League of Philadelphia**
121 S Broad St # 9,
Philadelphia, PA 19107
215-985-3220
www.urbanleaguephila.org

**The Jack Welch Management Institute at Strayer University**
2303 Dulles Station Blvd.
Herndon, VA 20171
855-596-5964

www.jackwelch.strayer.edu

# BIO

Tanya T. Morris is an author, speaker and mentor. She has impacted the lives of single women, ex-offenders and small business owners for nearly twenty years through mentoring, coaching and community engagement. She has transformed their lives personally, financially and professionally. Under her tutelage, many have started successful businesses, purchased their first homes and increased their income. Tanya T. has been prominently featured in various publications including *Speaker,* the publication of the National Speakers Association, the *Philadelphia Tribune, Philadelphia Sunday Sun* and others. Tanya T. has been featured on **WURD Radio**, **6ABC's Visions**, **KYW's News 3** and **NBC10**. She has also received the Pennsylvania Public Utility Commission's Utility Wise Community Service Award.

Searching for purpose, Tanya worked as a temporary employee and an administrator. When a friend asked her to do a workshop on communications at a halfway house for offenders, Tanya found her passion, motivational speaking. Tanya T. helps struggling entrepreneurs and transitionals increase productivity, reach their goals and achieve success in business and in life. She has a M.A. in Professional and Business Communication and an MBA in Executive Leadership.

Tanya@ThePoweroftheT.com
www.ThePoweroftheT.com

# RECOMMENDED READING

***Divine Inspirations: The Process of Fulfilling Your Divine Destiny***
Tanya T. Morris

***Drop Your Baggage: The Just Get Over It Makeover***
Tanya T. Morris

***Step Into Greatness Journal***
Nehemiah Davis

**Significant! From Frustrated to Franne-Tastic: Inspirational Stories for the Entrepreneurial Woman**
Franne McNeal

www.ingramcontent.com/pod-product-compliance
Lightning Source LLC
Chambersburg PA
CBHW071128090426
42736CB00012B/2050